Written by Sue Graves
Illustrated by Alison Atkins (John Martin & Artists)
Designed by Blue Sunflower Creative

Language consultant: Betty Root

This is a Parragon Publishing book
This edition published in 2004

Parragon Publishing
Queen Street House
4 Queen Street
Bath, BA1 1HE, UK

ISBN 1-40541-864-8
Printed in China

Who's in the Jungle?

p

Notes for Parents

Reading with your child is an enjoyable and rewarding experience. These **Gold Stars** reading books encourage and support children who are learning to read.

The **Gold Stars** reading books are filled with fun stories, familiar vocabulary, and amusing pictures. Sharing these books with your child will ensure that reading is fun. It is important, at this early stage, for children to enjoy reading and succeed. Success creates confidence.

Starting to read

Start by reading the book aloud to your child, taking time to talk about the pictures. This will help your child to see that pictures often give clues about the story.

Over a period of time, try to read the same book several times so that your child becomes familiar with the story and the words and phrases. Then your child will be ready to read the book aloud with you. It helps to run your finger under the words as you say them.

Occasionally, stop and encourage your child to continue reading aloud without you. Join in again when your child needs help. This is the next step toward helping your child become an independent reader.

Finally, your child will be ready to read alone. Listen carefully to your child and give plenty of praise. Remember to make reading an enjoyable experience.

Using your Gold Stars stickers

You can use the **Gold Stars** stickers at the back of the book as a reward for effort as well as achievement. Learning to read is an exciting challenge for every child.

Remember these four important stages:

- Read the story **to** your child.
- Read the story **with** your child.
- Encourage your child to read **to you**.
- Listen to your child read **alone**.

Look in the jungle.

Who can you see?

Can you see a lion under the tree?

"Roar, roar!" goes Lion.

Look in the jungle.

Who can you see?

Can you see an elephant
under the tree?

"Trump, trump!"
goes Elephant.

Look in the jungle.

Who can you see?

Can you see a crocodile
under the tree?

"Snap, snap!" goes
Crocodile.

Look in the jungle.

Who can you see?

Can you see a monkey
sitting in the tree?

"Yum, yum!" goes Monkey.
"What a tasty banana!"

Look in the jungle.

Who can you see?

It's a monkey, running as fast as can be!

Look back in your book. Can you find these words?

jungle

lion

elephant

crocodile

monkey

banana

29

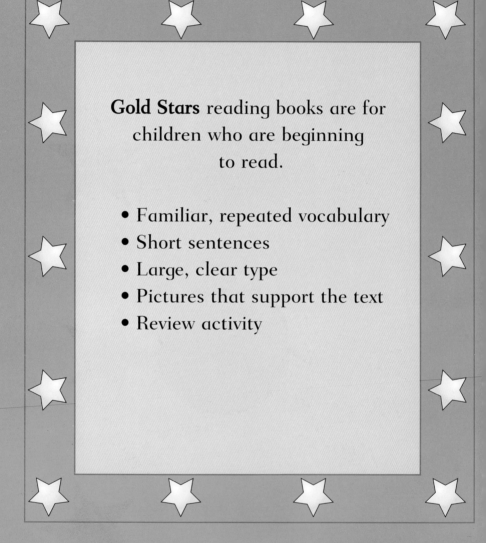

Gold Stars reading books are for children who are beginning to read.

- Familiar, repeated vocabulary
- Short sentences
- Large, clear type
- Pictures that support the text
- Review activity